Mediterranean Houses
Côte d'Azur and Provence

Editorial Gustavo Gili, S.A.

08029 Barcelona Rosselló, 87-89
Spain
Tel. (343) 322 81 61   Fax (343) 322 92 05

1st edition: 1991
2nd edition: 1993

Translation: Graham Thomson

All rights reserved. No part of this work covered by the copyright hereon may be reproduced or used in any form or by any means −graphic, electronic, or mechanical, including photocopying, recording, taping, or information storage and retrieval systems− without written permission of the publisher.

© Editorial Gustavo Gili, S.A., Barcelona, 1991

ISBN: 84-252-1552-8
Printed in Singapore by Star Standard Industries Pte. Ltd.

Mediterranean Houses
Côte d'Azur and Provence

Pascal Chossegros

**Photographies
Nicolas Borel**

GG®

Acknowledgments

My sincere thanks to all of the people who have contributed in one way or another to making this book a reality.

In view of the impossibility of mentioning them all by the name, I would like to express here my gratitude to every one of the owners of the houses dealt with, and also to the architects and their collaborators. My thanks in particular to Juliet Bréant for her invaluable assistance.

All of the photographs were specially taken for this book by Nicolas Borel, with the exception of those by Hughes Bigo (bottom of p. 11 and p. 18) and the photographs from the archives of the Musée des Arts Décoratifs-Editions A. Levy, Paris (top, b&w, pp. 36 and 37). The plans reproduced on pages 30 and 34 are from the book by Briolle/Fuzibet/Monnier –*La Ville Noailles*, Editions Parèntheses, Marseille, 1990. The plans reproduced on page 26 have been redrawn from photographs of the original plans provided by the Fondation Le Corbusier.

Contents

Acknowledgments	6
Introduction	10
Gibbs House, Lioux, Vaucluse. Gilles Bouchez. 1973	20
Villa de Mandrot, Pradet, Var. Le Corbusier. 1929-1931	26
Villa Noailles, Hyères, Var. Rob Mallet-Stevens. 1923-1933	30
Private house, Cap Bénat, Var. Philip Johnson. 1964	38
"Le Pas de Pique" villa, Le Tignet, Alpes-Maritimes. Marcel Lods. 1963	44
Germain swimming pool, Giens peninsula, Var. Roland Simounet. 1976	48
Unal house and studio, Ruoms, Ardèche. Claude and Pascal Hauserman. 1973	52
Bruyère house, Maussane, Bouches-du-Rhône. André Bruyère. 1971	58
"Adonaljo" house, Prades le Lez, Hérault. Yves Collet. 1985	62
Joly house ("La Bergère"), Roussillon, Vaucluse. Christophe Huet. 1989	68
Confino house ("Le Passe-Muraille"), Malataverne, Gard. François Confino. 1985	76
"La Petite Maison" house, Grasse, Alpes-Maritimes. Kristian Gullichsen. 1972	82
Doussot house, Bandol, Var. Rudy Ricciotti. 1987	86
Mancini house, Marseille, Bouches-du-Rhône. C.C.D. (Gérard Cerrito, Xavier Chabrol, Régis Daniel). 1984	90
Private house, Caseneuve, Vaucluse. Emmanuelle Colboc. 1987	96
Sauzet house, Sanary, Var. Maurice Sauzet. 1975	102
Coppens house, Bandol, Var. Rudy Ricciotti. 1988	106
Jaubert house, Pélissanne, Bouches-du-Rhône. Gaston Jaubert. 1970	112
"Arakao" house, Roussillon, Vaucluse. Jacques Gautier. 1985	116
Mahaux house, Nice, Alpes-Maritimes. Rudy Ricciotti. 1988	122
Gleize house, Nimes, Gard. François Clavel. 1982	128
Private house, Castelnau-le-Lez, Hérault. Guy Grégori. 1982	134
Private house, Toulon, Var. Roland Simounet. 1975	138

Introduction

Le Corbusier, Unité d'habitation, Marseille, 1946.

Georges-Henri Pingusson, Hôtel Latitude 43, Saint Tropez, 1931-1932

Leaving all stylistic debate aside, the Mediterranean architectures of south-eastern France – within the category of the private house presented here – are very solidly anchored in the spirit, the genius of the place.

It is for this reason that we have chosen to structure this text in terms of specific themes, which we consider to be more descriptive of this architecture, such as sun, water, colour, materials and vegetation. Nevertheless, without being unduly pedantic, it was apparent that certain projects were the product of an organic architecture, while others belonged within the modernist tradition. Their universal signature would be equally at home in many other parts of the Mediterranean.

On the other hand, a regionalist modernism fed by the sense of place – which would not have been disavowed by those masters of the Modern Movement who had occasion to build on the Côte d'Azur – seems to characterise south-eastern France. Adapted to each individual site, this architecture assumes its place in the contemporary world without violence, with a gentle yet sustained presence, which adjusts to particular local building regulations without lapsing into pastiche. Thus the autonomy of the architectural object acquiesces in its disappearance.

The constant of climate is certainly a recurring element in Mediterranean architecture. Whatever the geology, the landscape or the relationship with the sea, the presence of the sun shapes the built structure. The subtle detail of the towns of northern Europe (the elaborate brickwork, the finely sculpted cornises,...) which shine with a soft grey light would be meaningless in the Mediterranean world. The sun flattens the perspective of volumes to reduce everything to the interplay of solid and void, mass and opening.

Elements designed to give shelter from the sun, such as arcades, verandas and *brise-soleil* screens, together with closed exterior spaces such as courtyards, contribute significantly to the typology of the Mediterranean environment on the Côte d'Azur.

At the end of the last century, the aristocracy would visit Nice, Cannes or Monaco in winter, as a precaution

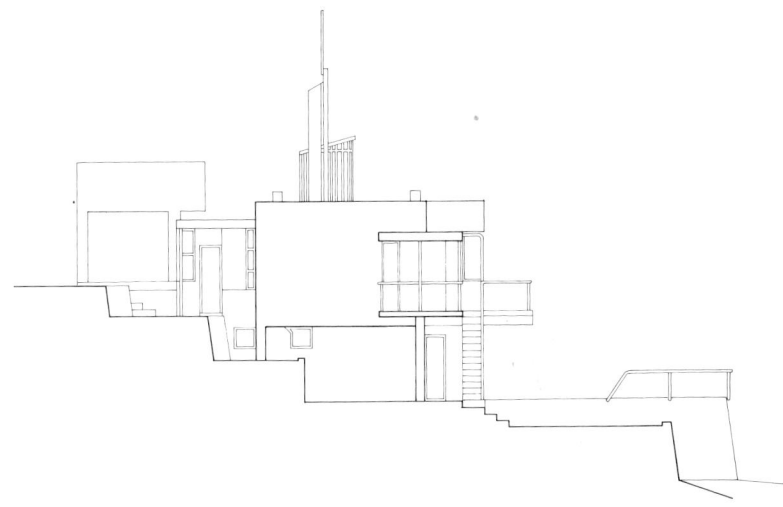

Eileen Gray, west facade of the Villa E 1027, Cap-Martin, 1927.

General view of Cap-Martin: in the foreground, Eileen Gray's Villa E 1027; above and to the rear, the camping *unités*, "L'Étoile de mer" and Le Corbusier's cabin.

against exposure to the sun. It took Mademoiselle Chanel, in tandem with the Modern Movement, to call into being a summer habitat, open to the sun, the sea, and outdoor sports.

These contemporary houses derive from that fact, existing in symbiosis with the environment and in opposition, for the most part, to the traditional construction of the Provençal farmhouse. That typology has been inverted, as a result of this century's radical change in styles of living, in the same way as the arrival of the elevator modified the stratification of the Paris apartment building.

It is possible that this relationship with the sun might be inverted once again with the discovery of such ills as skin cancer. A balanced moderation would spend the day alternating between sun and shade in a dialogue between ancestral values and those of the modern world.

The confrontation between modern architects and the Côte d'Azur has been a double one. Two major buildings with a nautical inspiration, the *Unité d'habitation* in Marseille (Le Corbusier) and Latitude 43 (G.H. Pingusson), paved the way for an uncompromising collective environment in the south-east. The concrete outer skin of the *Unité*, and that of the white-rendered Latitude, have served as guidelines for certain contemporary private houses (R. Simounet, R. Ricciotti, ...)

However, these architects' responses to the private habitat have emerged as humbler, more modest, and yet at the same time more complex. The reason for this probably lies in the power and the magic of the place. Pingusson's villas in Beauvallon, Le Corbusier's villa de Mandrot and cabin at Cap-Martin, Eileen Gray's villa Tempe in Pailla, the villa Noailles by R. Mallet-Stevens or the Vent d'Aval by P. Chareau, employ typically regional materials (wood, stone, traditional masonry), or a local typology (tiled roof, arcade), or colour to engage in a dialogue with the site over and above the stylistic debate of the period.

Alone, outside its context and quite unique, Eileen Gray's villa E 1027 stands on the Cap-Martin peninsula as a theoretical object, in parallel with A. Loos' 1923 project for a villa in Lavandou.

Le Corbusier died at Cap-Martin. His tomb by the sea will mark the site forever. Time passes, shapes the remains of the Modern Movement, then slowly erases them.

While the de Mandrot and Noailles villas are undergoing restoration, the buildings by E. Gray, G.H. Pingusson, the Marseille *Unité* and the cabin at Cap-Martin all show the ravages of time. They are not yet quite in ruins, but they are on their way to dissolving into the landscape. Although it is true that their systems of construction were intrinsically fragile, the seasonal, summer occupation of some of these buildings, and the lack of maintenance of others (the *unité d'habitation*) have contributed to their premature ageing. The effects of time here are symbolic. The modest horizons of architectural practice in the south-east over several decades, the reasons for which are cultural and historical, stem from an affected ignorance of the outstanding architectural examples left there by the Modern Movement. Vernacular regionalism, at best, or simple incompetence, have covered the Côte d'Azur and Provence with constructions devoid of architecture. The commissioning of foreign architects (N. Foster, R. Rogers, O. Bohigas, W. Alsop, M. Botta, ...), whether in Nimes, Marseille or Aix en Provence, represents the continuation of a tradition which seeks to give dynamism to local creativity by means of contributions from outside. Parallel to this, the emergence of studios run by young local architects seems to presage an architectural renaissasnce in an eternal Mediterranean where time stands still.

A large part of the port of Marseille was destroyed by bombing during the Second World War, notably in the outer suburb of the Mairie. Fernand Pouillon reconstructed an architecture of mortared stone here which structures the sunlit face of the Vieux Port.

An architecture of deep loggias on the upper floors and grand ground level arcades occupied by shops which recreates an intermediary space between the public and the private. This residential environment with its modern classicism, free of ornament, with its flat tiled roofs, is contemporary with Le Corbusier's *Cité Radieuse*. It proposes a regional, rational reading of some of the elements of the *unité* (loggias, arcades in place of pilotis, commercial premises integrated into a residential programme, ...).

A response to the growing demand for a second home, residential developments started to appear along the Côte d'Azur in the 1960s: Le Gaou Bénat (Aubert and Lefèvre), Castellaras le Neuf (J. Couelle), Port Grimaud (F. Spoerry). In Gaou Bénat the urban planning regulations imposed an architecture of strata which is perfectly integrated with the slopes of the Maures. All of the roads are underground, and the whole development vanishes into the shadows of the luxuriant vegetation. The houses are discreetly concealed about the site.

At Castellaras le Neuf, the sculptor and architect Jacques Couelle developed his own architecture of curving contours independently of prevailing styles. If his trogloditic houses with their surprising forms have inspired any kind of school, they have opened up a space for the curvilinear form which has gone on to be used, in fragmentary fashion, in numerous private houses.

At Port Grimaud, on what was formerly marshland, François Spoerry has created a marina in which the grouping of houses amidst squares and alleys, with a typology of stylistic collage, offers a nautical lifestyle. This piece of work, widely criticised at the time, is an undeniable success in commercial and spatial terms. Port Grimaud continues to develop under the aegis of its architect and urban designer. In parallel to these houses with their respect for the site, the coastline from Hérault to the Alpes-Maritimes has been marked by other more vertical projects and a denser environment, such as the Grande Motte (J. Baladur) or the Baie des Anges marina (M. Marot). From the privacy of traditional building to the deliberately architectural gesture, these constructions have been adapted to the economic imperatives inherent in each situation, leaving an unconscious yet evocative trace in the memory.

The recurring theme of this collection is Mediterranean architecture. Open to the sea, this architecture extends the marine aspect of the place through the presence of swimming pools, with the life of the summer residents being centred on the pool and the sea. The architecture

The port of Marseille
Castellaras le Neuf.

Gaou Bénat.
Port Grimaud.

seeks to disappear as an object, to become immaterial, opening itself up to provide views of the sea.

The swimming pools are a part of this landscape, a portion of the sea, appropriated and given over to everyday use, practical and readily accessible. The sea to be enjoyed in views is at the same time something to be directly experienced.

The curve of the beaches and the rolling, stormy sea, as well as the horizontal plane of the sea when calm, create a moving space which is watery, almost womblike. The swimming pool by R. Simounet, a balcony overlooking the sea, makes much of this duality of the marine element.

Surrounded by the swelling sea, coves, the curves and contours of the land and the vegetation, the desire for integration, to be part of the context, has led certain architects towards non-rectilinear projects, to reject the cerebral filter of the geometry of straight lines. In spite of the sculptural quality of these schemes, this is evidently a marginal response when it comes to generating the complete volumetry of the project (C. and P. Hauserman, J. Couelle, A. Lovag, …). Far removed from the construction aesthetic of A. Gaudí or J. Mª Pujol, or the reasoned coherence of Eero Saarinen (TWA terminal at JFK airport), this is a composite architecture, cavernous and animal.

On the other hand, the application of this curvilinar system within an orthogonal framework (A. Bruyère), or the undulating treatment of certain exteriors (R. Simounet, M. Sauzet) easily and felicitously links architecture and landscape. This latter aesthetic belongs, moreover, to the spirit of the time (rear facade of the Dance Theatre in The Hague by R. Koolhaas) in its rationalisation of the irregular logic of the curving line.

The whitewashed rendering of the houses of Greece or Ibiza confers an immaterial whiteness to their volumes. This luminous white can also be found in some of the buildings on the Croisette or the Promenade des Anglais. Pure and aseptic, it has been imported to the Côte d'Azur. A sign of the Modern Movement on the one hand, and evocative of other projects such as the Villa Kerylos by E. Pontremoli, its dual relationship is animated by its rapport with the setting. Its contemporary interpretation expresses a clear desire to integrate the exterior aspects of the building with the location. The dreamlike quality of this architecture marks and tends to exist for itself, over and above its context. A reflection of mechanisation, Promethean, it exists in a direct relationship with the Hegelian values. It remains modernist, at variance with an epoch marked by doubt, immaturity and lack of balance.

The geological base of some of the hills of Marseille, and the "bories" of the Lubéron –shepherds' shelters built of corbelled dry stone– are almost identical in substance and colour to the concrete of the Marseille *Unité*. Theoretically akin to white modernism, the house of concrete or concrete block reads very differently. It seems to blend into the rocky landscape, the shadows suddenly soften to tones of grey and the windows disappear.

Set down amidst the ochres of Roussillon, J. Gautier has created a house which seems to have grown up out of its setting. In similar fashion, the expressionist character of A. Lovag's building in Théoule-sur-mer is based on the reddish tonalities of the Esterel.

From the old town of Nice to the Galères quarter of Marseille, coloured renderings are a historical constant in the external treatment of urban buildings in the southeast, between the visible and perfectly proportioned Roman monuments of Saint-Rémi, Arles, Nimes or Orange and the industrial, mechanical proportions of the 19th century buildings. From surface pigmentation to pigment mixed into the plaster or the glazed roof (R. Ricciotti), the expressive uses of colour have been adapted to the character and personality of the individual architect.

This architecture of colour shines out in the sunlight between the natural blues of sea and sky and those of the swimming pools. Certain roofs, window shutters (C.C.D.), a bathroom (F. Clavel), use blue, absorbing and returning here and there the primordial elements. This is a Moslem Mediterranean (the Blue Mosque in Istanbul) which has been evoked perhaps unconsciously. On a more prosaic note, it calls to mind the traditional blue and white checkered pattern common in local tiled floors.

Swimming pool surrounds in teak or Iroko wood (C.C.D., R. Ricciotti, ...), stone (F. Confino) or tiles (M. Sauzet) – local or imported materials and techniques – are to be found in discreet exteriors, no doubt from a desire to express a certain modernism or from a concern with standing out from the surrounding mediocrity of contemporary vernacular architecture. By contrast, these materials find their place in the interiors of this environment. The clients, prompted by the wish to experience a Mediterranean way of life, to be grounded in local tradition, have chosen them in order to counterbalance the modern aesthetic of the exterior. The day-to-day life of the occupants has had a moderating influence on the rigour of architectural theories.

The vertical lines of the cypress trees and the horizontals of the umbrella pines and the sea frame the views of the landscape in an orthogonal system, an intimation of the infinite which encourages reverie. By contrast, the curving contours of an undulating landscape, the vivid angles of the rock (G. Jaubert) and the supple mass of the undergrowth anchor the spirit to the earth.

It is between these two opposing conditions that Mediterranean architecture has had to find its existence. The adopting of architectural positions has followed the same approach, whether it be through integrating and domesticating nature (garden by G. Guévrekian, villa by M. Sauzet), through ignoring it (villas by R. Ricciotti), or through the enveloping and dematerialising of the building by nature (villa by Gullichsen). The force and presence of the Mediterranean landscape is a constant which interacts with the architecture and gives it its individual character. The sense of microcosm created by the surrounding vegetation of some of these gardens, a fringe between the building and the landscape, is symptomatic of the powerful presence of the landscape on these sites.

This catalogue of contemporary private houses in the south-east of France cannot claim to be impartial or exhaustive. The process of selection – bearing in mind the inherent interest of the architecture – has been guided above all by a desire for diversity and a rejection of prejudice. We felt it was necessary to present some examples of work which stands outside modernism, since this evidently reflects a reality and a need.

At the same time we have sought to break away from the specificity of building in this region by rapport with other Mediterranean buildings where– while certain constants such as climate, the presences of sea and landscape remain– it is the individual qualities of the place, its history and culture, that give them their particular character.

At the same time, however, we have deliberately excluded regionalist pastiche, which is adequately represented in its own publications, and stands on the fringes of architectural debate.

Pascal Chossegros, architect

Le Corbusier's cabin, Cap-Martin, 1950.

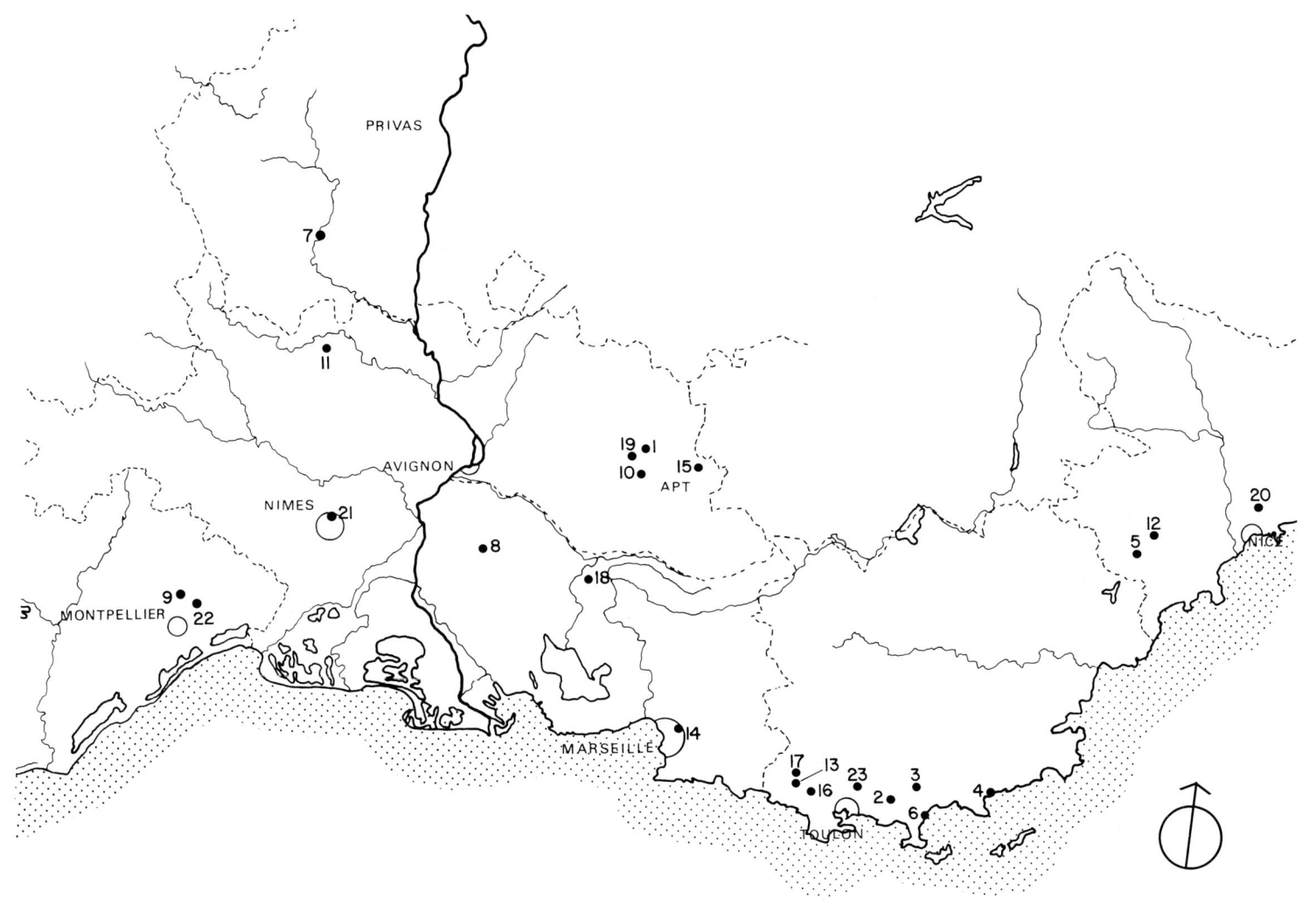

1 Gibbs house
2 Villa de Mandrot
3 Villa Noailles
4 Private house
5 "Le Pas de Pique" villa
6 Germain swimming pool
7 Unal house and studio
8 Bruyère house
9 "Adonaljo" house
10 Joly house ("La Bergère")
11 Confino house ("Le Passe-Muraille")
12 "La Petite Maison" house
13 Doussot house
14 Mancini house
15 Private house
16 Sauzet house
17 Coppens house
18 Jaubert house
19 "Arakao" house
20 Mahaux house
21 Gleize house
22 Private house
23 Private house

Gibbs house

Gilles Bouchez
Lioux. Vaucluse, 1973
212 m²
Brick, concrete, terracotta.

In spite of everything, it is curious to consider the poor response to solar energy –passive or active– in France. The south-east, with its exceptional sunshine, would seem in principle to be an ideal place for this technology.

The specificity of the technology and the small number of firms with expertise in the field, together with its innovative character, are probably the main reasons for the lack of interest in and development of solar power in the south-east. This solar-powered house uses air as a transmitter of heat. A 52 m² collector traps the warm air, and a 30 m³ mass of pebbles in the filter bed is used to store it. The introverted plan of the atrium is made up of 4 units connected by an external circulation route and opens to the south.

The regular, highly organised geometry reveals certain Kahnian qualities, while at the same time the laying out of the volumes around a central courtyard recalls a number of Tony Garnier's projects (villas in Cassis, Saint-Chavond, ...)

The way the views of the landscape are focussed, and the richness and quality of the light, give the house a character all its own.

Site plan, sections and views of the exterior.

21

Various views of the porch and the terrace.

23

Views of the exterior, the entrance and the interior.

Villa de Mandrot

Le Corbusier
Pradet, Var, 1929-1931
150 m²
Limestone walls, with brick partitions, reinforced concrete pillars, floor of hexagonal red tiles, plywood ceiling.

This house was designed by Le Corbusier for the woman who founded the CIAM in the Sarraz.

In consideration of the fact that the modernist revolution was well under way, Le Corbusier is concerned first and foremost in this project with the volume, the surface and the plan, and only subsequently with the materials.

The L-shaped plan is composed of 6 square volumes with sides of 3.90 m, separated by intervals of 0.45 m.

A separate guests' bedroom and two groups of bedrooms (for the owner and her domestic staff) which open onto the kitchen, together with an enormous living room comprise the main floor. A basement studio completes the programme.

Two statues by Lipchitz punctuate the exterior space.

The house is exclusively south-facing. A number of problems with the house were the subject of an extended correspondence between client and architect which led to repair work which was finally completed in 1936.

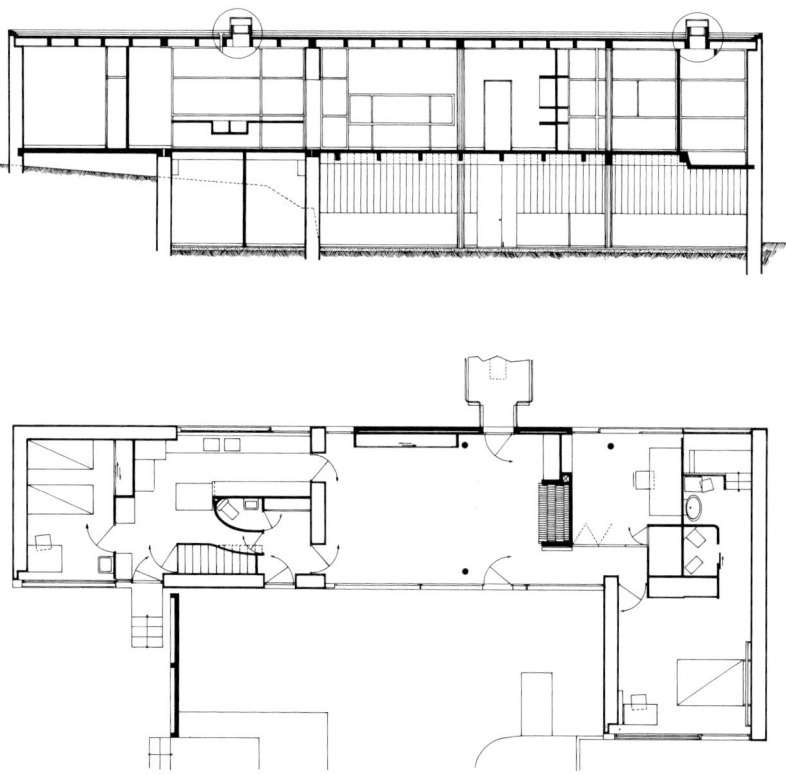

Section, plan and general view of the house from the entrance.

Views of the garden and the guests' pavilion.

Villa Noailles

Rob Mallet-Stevens
Hyères, Var, 1923-1933
1800 m²
Walls of small chalky local stones, floors resting on iron I-beams and brickwork, iron I-section lintels infilled with concrete, concrete elements, terrazo floor, grey roughcast, glass paving slabs.

Standing at the foot of the ruins of the old château, this villa is one of Rob Mallet-Stevens first built schemes. The interior decoration was carried out by T. Van Doesburg, P. Chareau, F. Jourdain and G. Djo-Bourgeois, amongst others. The vicomte Noailles was involved at every stage of the construction, modelling the project around the functional utility he wanted from the villa.

The villa was designed to be used during the winter. Subsequent extensions, to which Mallet-Stevens did not contribute (garden by Guevrékian, statue by Lipchitz, glass ceiling by Barillet, swimming pool, gymnasium, squash court, ...) provided for a château lifestyle based around the arts and sport. L. Buñuel and Man Ray stayed at the villa, where they made two films (*Les mystères de Château de Dé* and *L'age d'or*).

The house is now used as the town of Hyères' international encounter and creativity centre.

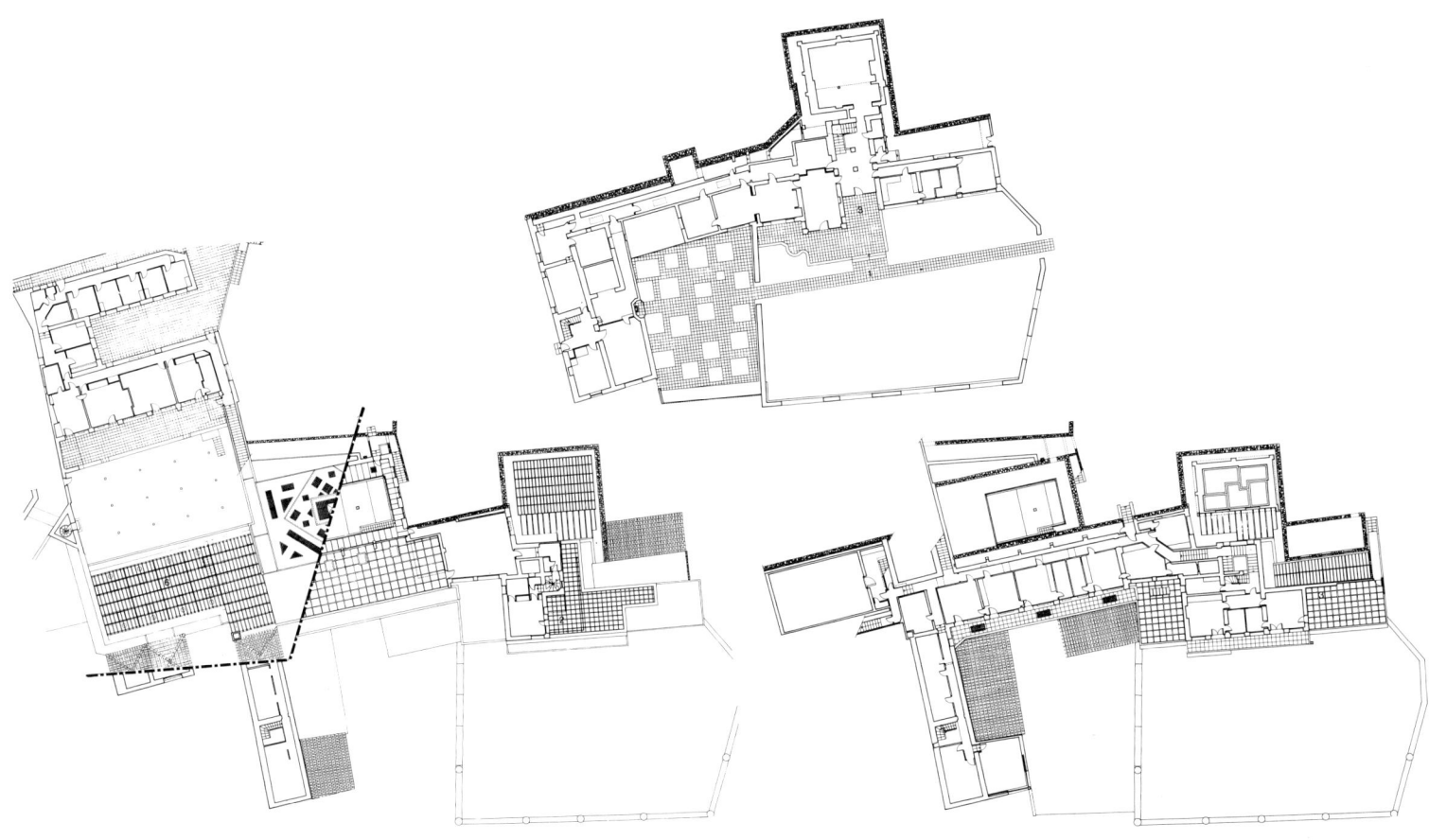

Plans and details of the exterior.

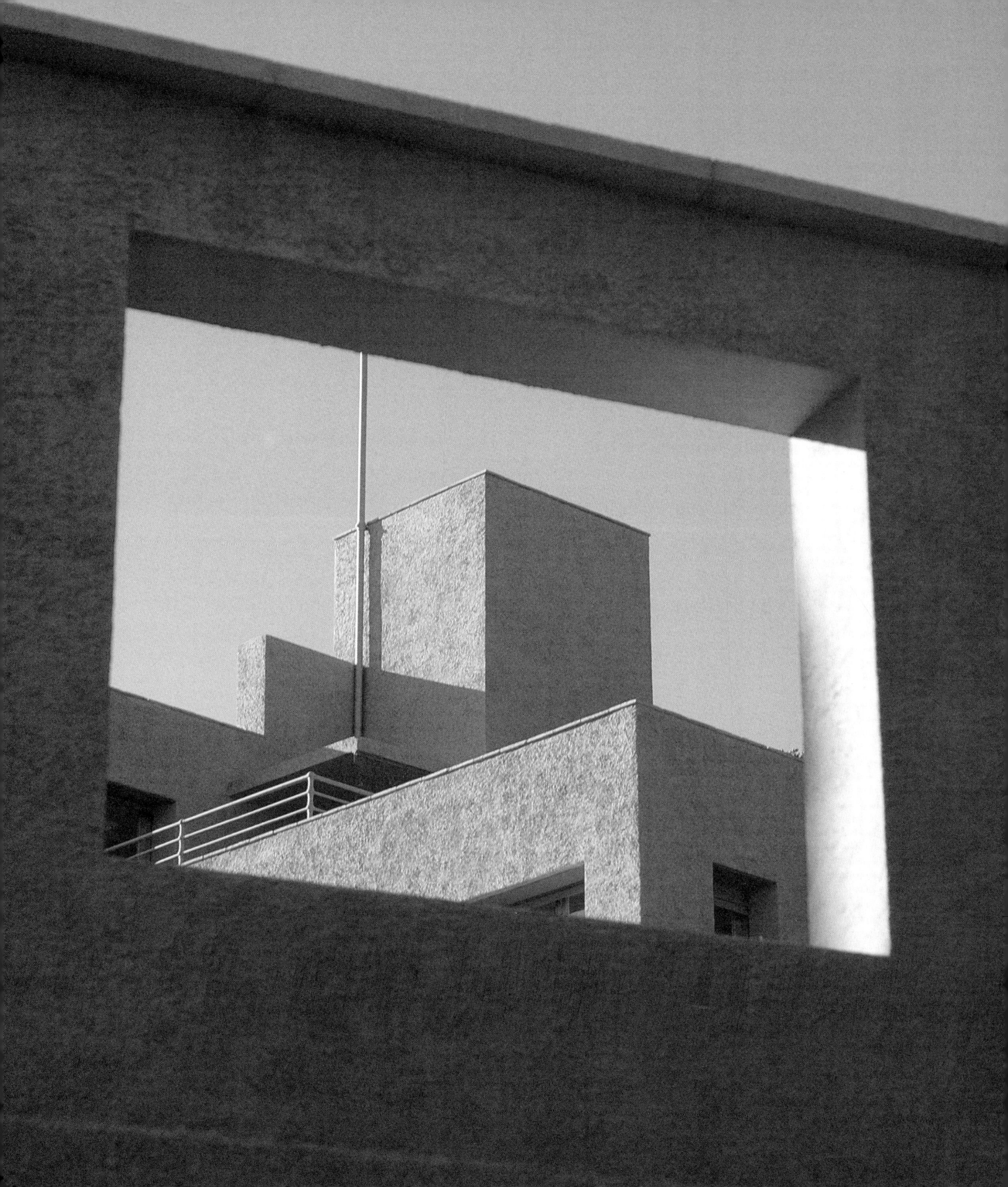

Views of the exterior and the garden.

Plan and photographs of the triangular garden designed by Gabriel Guévrékian (1926) and view of the terrace and the "chambre en plein air" designed by Pierre Chareau (1928).

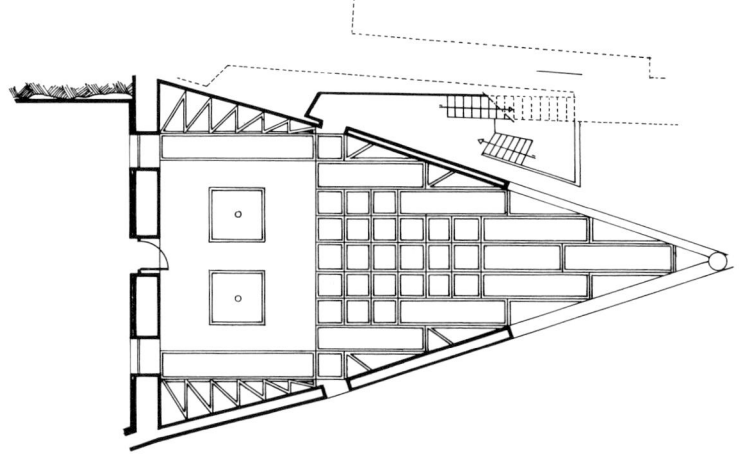

Views of the dining room as it is now, and in 1928, with the furniture designed by G. Djo-Bourgeois.

Views of Charles de Noailles' studio as it is now and in 1928.

37

Private house

Philip Johnson
Cap Bénat, Var, 1964
321 m²

The outstanding feature of this house is the unique beauty of its position, surrounded by pinewoods, and set high above the sea on the brow of a hill dominating the entire coastline and offering a wide panorama towards south and east. It consists of five self-contained dwelling units and serves mainly as a holiday home for a large family, although it is equipped with all the facilities required for permanent residence. The design has exploited the entire site. To a much greater extent than usual, the outdoor areas have become integrated with the internal ones. The boundaries between different areas are defined not by walls or ceilings but by the floors. On the north side, the living room is screened by two rubble walls. The centre of the complex is the covered patio which serves to link the central part, the living room and one of the dwelling units. The shell roof of the patio, composed of hyperparabolic panels, is supported by four sturdy tapering columns. The dwelling units all have a projecting reinforced concrete framework with non-structural panels which are plastered at ground floor level.

Site plan, plan and view of the exterior and the surroundings.

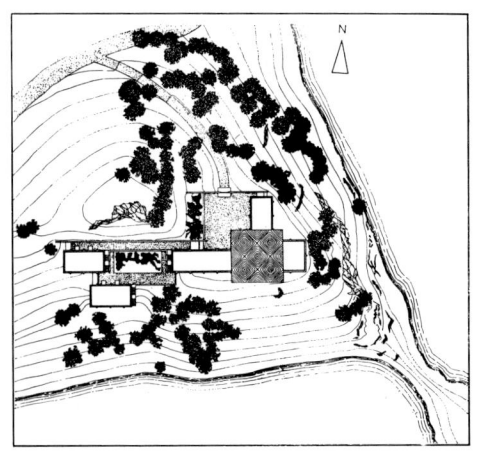
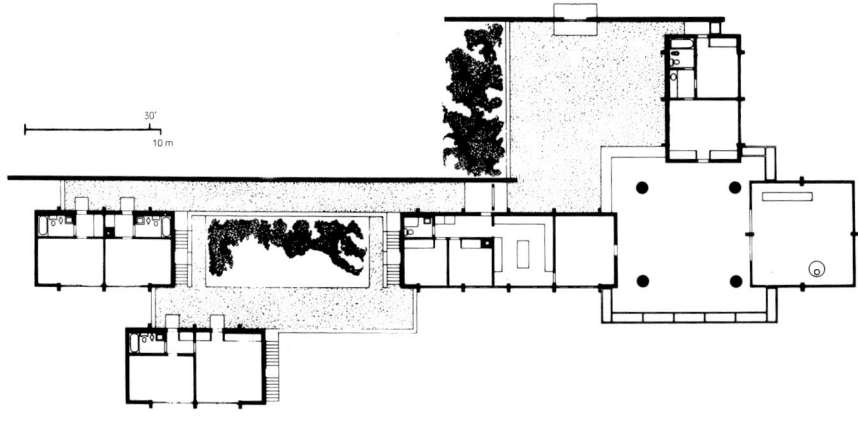

Various views of the roofed terrace.

Living room, entrance and view of the west facade.

"Le Pas de Pique", villa

Marcel Lods
Le Tignet, Alpes-Maritimes, 1963
110 m²
Load-bearing metal structure, wood partitions.

The spare conception of this building and its precision reveal more "of the technique of the automobile than that of the building".

This is one of the few examples of a metal structure presented here.

In fact, M. Lods was one of the first to use industrial metal systems in France, which he has applied here to the construction of his own house. Standing on a promontory, this house consists of a service area (kitchen, bathrooms) to the north and a large open space (bedroom, office, living room) to the south.

The construction on pilotis is another singular feature of the house. This practice, somewhat unusual in the south-east – Le Corbusier's *unités de camping* for Rebutato at Cap-Martin being another, earlier example – has here been adapted extremely well to a steeply sloping site. One would have to look to Los Angeles ("building the slope" by D. Rouillard) to find the same idea developed, and the same spatial effects transcribed. The economy it has brought to the project and the lightness it has conferred on the volume and the structure have made this house a reference point.

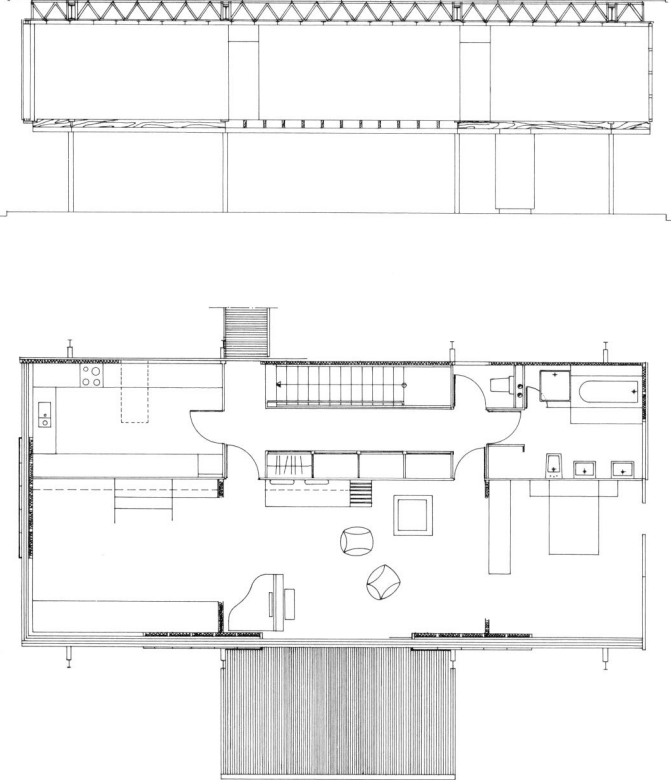

Section, plan and views of the main facade and its surroundings.

Views of the terrace, the belvedere, the living room and panoramic view from the living room and the terrace.

Germain swimming pool

Roland Simounet
Giens peninsula, Var, 1976
400 m² (water area 140 m²)
Concrete, rendering, stone.

   Soft and enclosed, this swimming pool merges into the landscape in skilful curves. The delicacy of the treatment of the access highlights this swimming pool on a promontory, and the walls which frame the landscape are equally indefinite. These vary in height between 500 mm and 1240 mm. The adroit interplay of forms makes this the antithesis of those large pools abounding in orthogonal rigidity. There is a lyrical and organic quality to the modelling of the materials. The space itself is a recreation of the sea's movements – the rocks against which the sea crashes are here become vague. The dynamic of the spatial treatment contrasts with the tranquility of the water's surface, sheltered from the wind. This microcosm of the two states of the sea, between calm and agitation, presents an architecture in tension within a limited space, a reflection of contemporary cosmology. Between paradise lost and the violence of our world, it might recall the garden of the Lante villa in Bagnia.

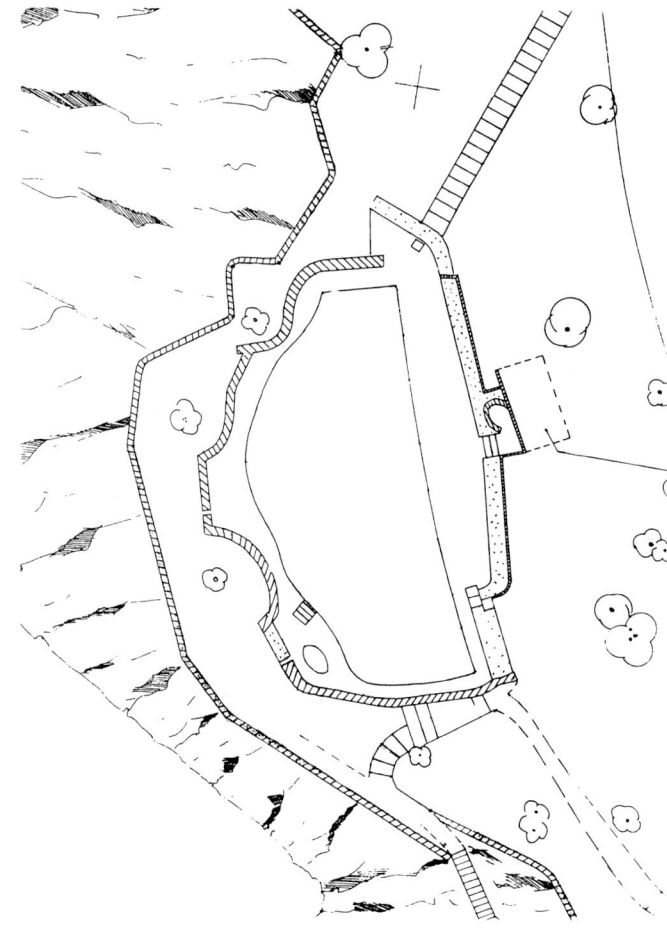

Sketch, plan and detail of the boundary wall.

Various views of the swimming pool and the boundary wall.

Unal house and studio

Claude and Pascal Hauserman
Ruoms, Ardèche, 1973
260 m²
Cast projecting concrete.

This house, built by the owners themselves, is remarkable in that in a sense it has more to do with sculpture than architecture. From Cheval's ideal palace to Paolo Soleri's self-built house, this living architecture develops the theme of the circle. Around the rooms of the two brothers whose house this is, a studio, a child's room and a room for the parents – located on the first floor – propose a hedonistic lifestyle between the courtyard and the water-tank. The functions of everyday life intersect in the volume, creating a flexible, moving space. The resulting external form comes together around the verticals of the two chimneys. The shelter and nourishment provided by this timeless building recall the primitive rural dwellings of the Palaeolithic, between Altamira and Lascaux.

Plan, sections and detail of the exterior.

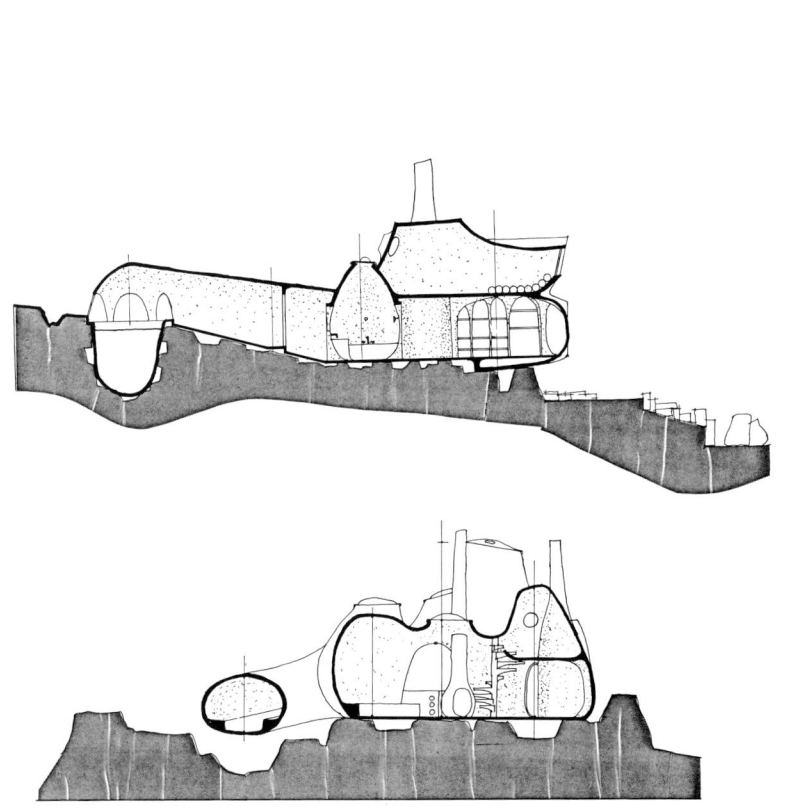
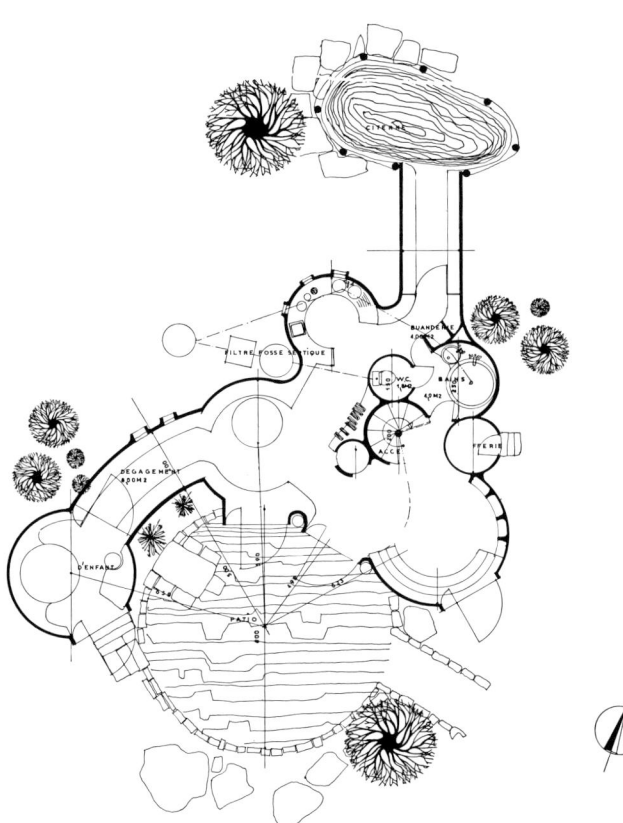

Previous pages: partial views of the exterior and the entrance.

Views of the interior.

Bruyère house

André Bruyère
Maussane, Bouches-du-Rhône, 1971
233 m²
Concrete beams, precast concrete floor units,
rendered concrete blocks.

Three volumes, main house, studio and house for guests, garage and table-tennis room, inhabited hangars, "shaping tenderness from constraint". The organisation of the main volume is composed of recesses, mysteries, double functions which dissolve the conventional divisions of the living environment. Its isolation and the rendered walls keep this modern house cool in summer. The vaults have been left in their rough state, showing the marks of the construction process. This house is built in direct contact with the ground, without a suspended floor, communing with nature. The drawing tables around the edge of the living room and the architect's bedroom serve to recall that this holiday residence is also a place of work. The multiple seating gives a special quality to the characteristic spaces of the living room, grouped around the fireplace or a courtyard. The openings to the exterior are minimal – with the exception of the large bay giving onto the courtyard –, thus conserving the intimate and inward-looking character of the house.

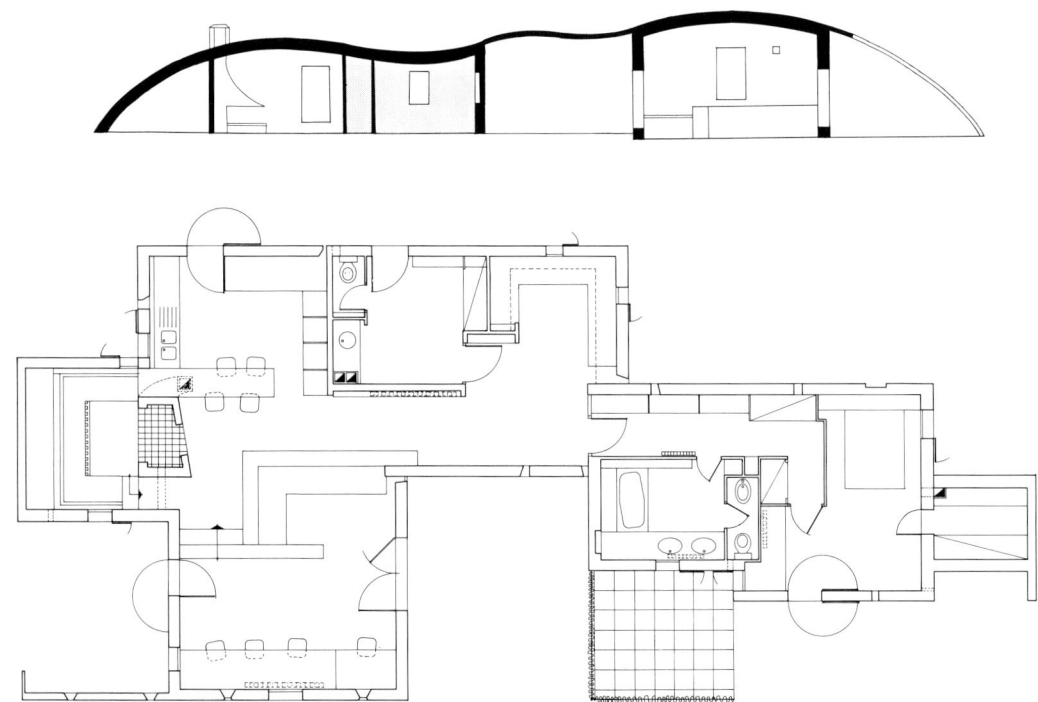

Section of the main building, plan and views of the exterior and the surroundings.

Views of the rear facade, the roof, the swimming pool, the courtyard and view of the study-living room.

"Adonaljo" house

Yves Collet
Prades le Lez, Hérault, 1985
210 m²
Concrete, smooth-finished rendered masonry.

Intersection of volumes to create a dwelling with modernist overtones.
The house is part of a development constructed by Yves Collet. On the ground floor an extensive programme – bedroom, living room, kitchen, bathrooms, dining room – occupies the entire space. On the first floor, an exterior staircase gives access to the central terrace flanked by the two volumes. The almost non-existent openings on the entrance facade are multiplied on the side facades, to open out with spacious bays on the main facade. Two terraces on the ground floor – one roofed, the other open but delimited by a system of posts and beams – offer spaces for relaxation at different times of year. The geometrical organisation combines the symmetry of the rear facade with indentations to allow the development of the main facade. An archway characterises the dining room. The privileged location frames views of the surrounding landscape from the large fireplace in the living room.

Plans and view of the exterior.

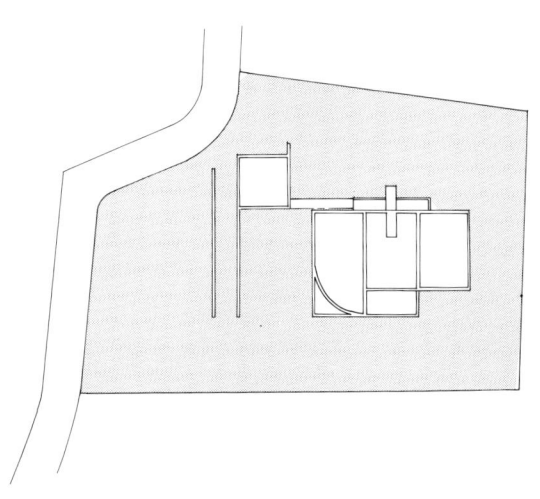 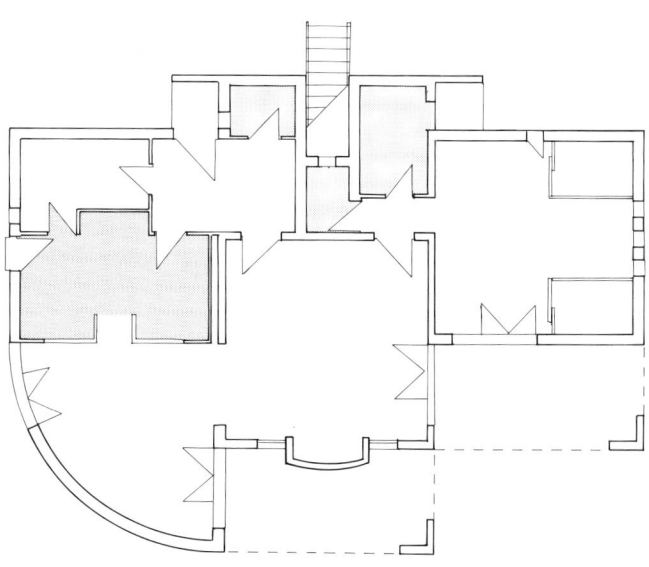

Various views of the exterior.

Following pages: partial views of the exterior and views of the interior.

Joly house ("La Bergère")

Christophe Huet
Roussillon, Vaucluse, 1989
164 m²
Roughcast and partition walls, stone and fitted carpets on the floor.

An object set down in the landscape, the mass of this house is perforated by transparencies. A portico and prominent free-standing walls shelter the volume and mark a transition in the environment.

The space is organised in a singular fashion, with the bedrooms and kitchen opening onto the living room. A slanting lightwell divides the house into two parts – the public area and the main space. This room receives its pale northern light from the windows of the bathroom and the mezzanine overlooking it. The bath is placed against the glazed facade with a theatrical attention to setting.

To the south, where the garden is laid out, the house overhangs the site. The use of light, with the glazed window bays of the main bedroom and the living room, the small openings on the other three facades and the stained glass windows over the stairs, creates an effect of contrast.

A dual orthogonality clearly marks the different parts of the programme and their respective treatments.

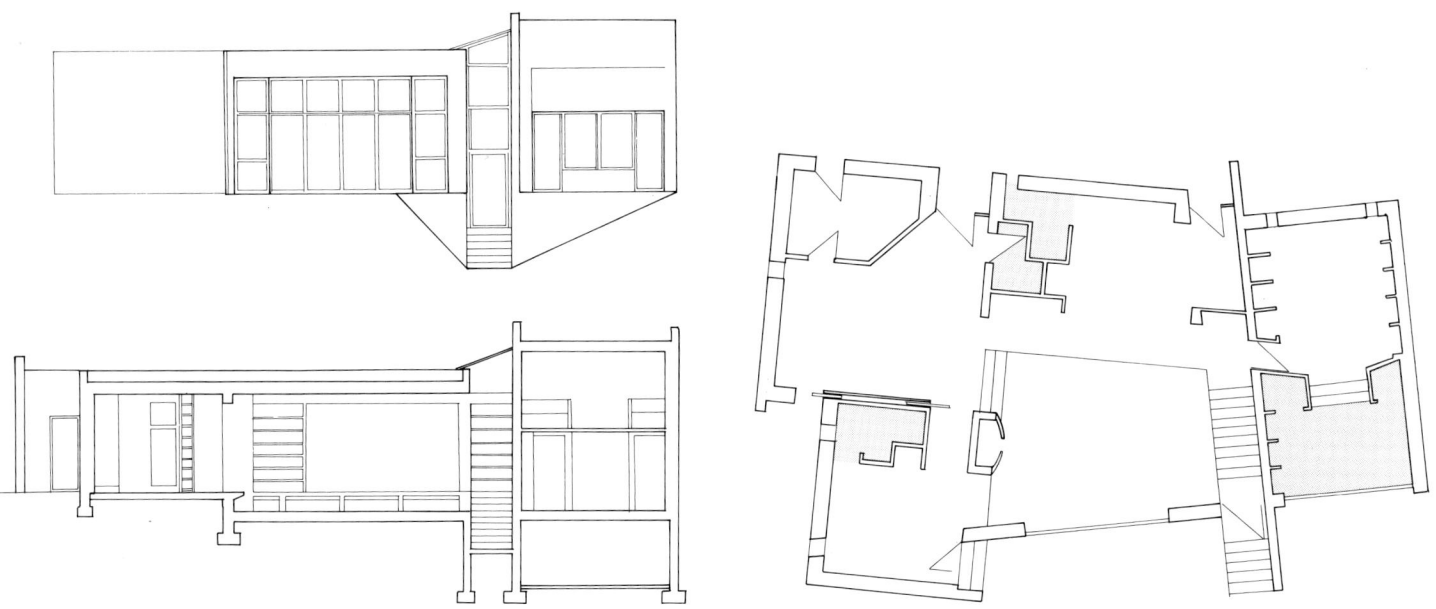

Elevation, section, plan and view of the main facade.

View of the rear facade.

View of the living room from the exterior.

Details of the exterior.

Detail of the interior balcony and views of the interior.

Confino house ("Le Passe-Muraille")

François Confino
Malataverne, Gard, 1985
160 m²
Existing undressed stone, metal, partition walls.

The success of this intervention within an existing context is due to the balance between integration and new design scheme. The project combines different materials to create a theatrical atmosphere.

The ruin on the edge of the cliff, which serves as the underpinning for the project, has been whitewashed. This is dominated by a roof terrace which conceals the house from view. The house opens to the south, overlooking the plain. The landscaping has allowed the natural rock to predominate. A large archway set against the hill encircles the space. A fragmented composition of glazed partitions encloses the house to the south. A structure of cylindrical pillars, interior and exterior, enlarges both the field of vision and the volume of the house. The bays thus become immaterial and the boundary between house and landscape disappears.

The path giving access passes through a circle of rocks and the surrounding wall winds round to conceal the landscape from view, to reveal it to even greater effect once the threshold has been crossed.

The name of the house, "Le Passe Muraille", is taken from a novel by Marcel Aymé whose central character physically crosses the walls. A statue to the left of the entrance recalls the book.

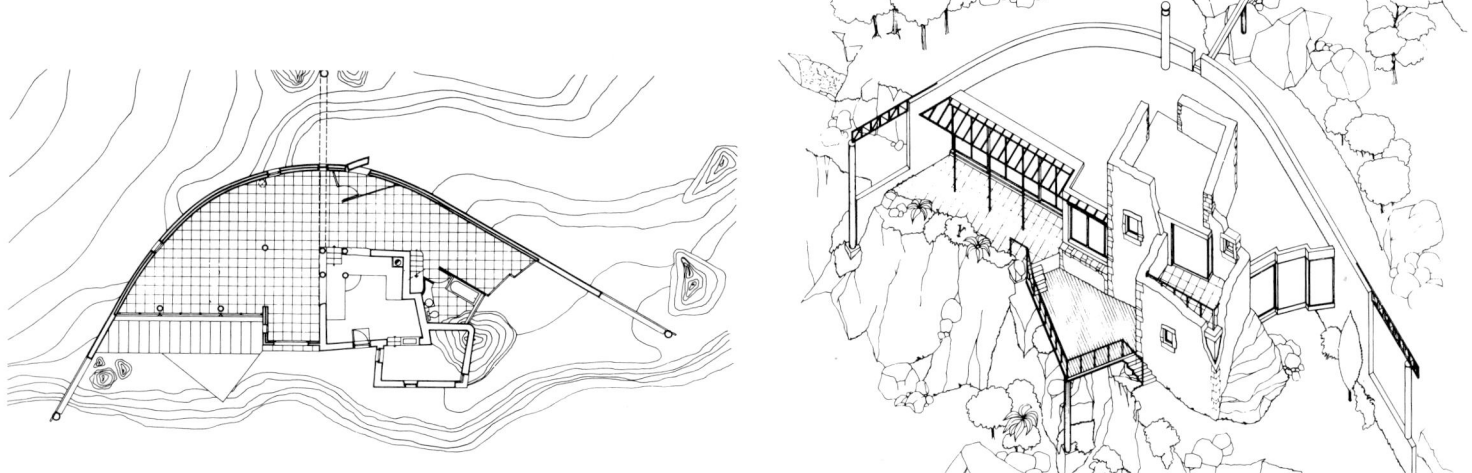

Plan, axonometric and views of the exterior.

Partial views of the exterior.

Detail of the exterior, views of the interior and view of the porch.

"La Petite Maison" house

Kristian Gullichsen
Grasse, Alpes-Maritimes, 1972
Wood, stone.

This uni-directional house is literally supported by its site. It is humble, invisible and open to the sun.

"This little house built for my mother, was designed to integrate into the landscape of the south of France. The stepped slope of the site was already there, all that was needed was to let the house down onto one of the cultivated terraces of little olives groves.

There is no main entrance – all of the rooms occupy a single disorganised structure looking onto the main space, the neighbouring terrace and the bucolic Mediterranean landscape.

This is a very intimate little house, closer to the way of life of a modern-day Diogenes than to formal society: it is entirely private."

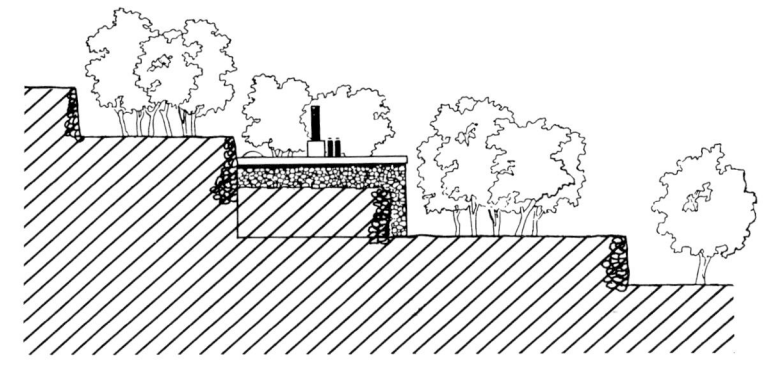

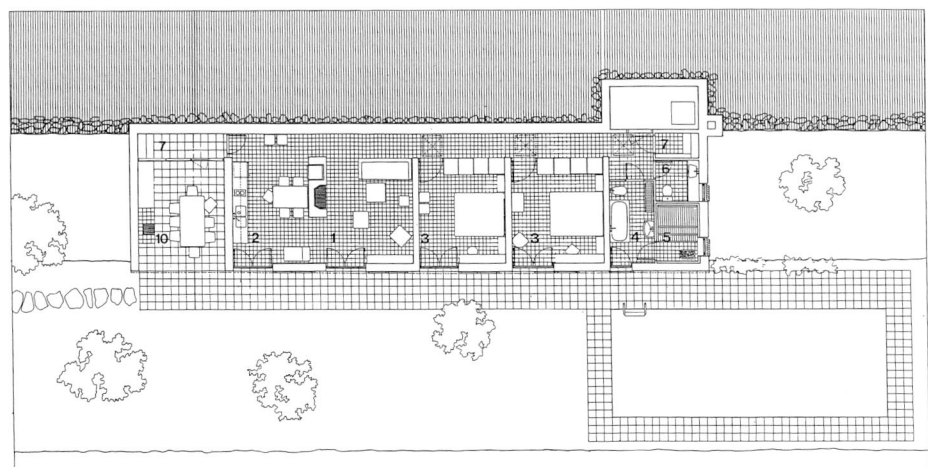

Section, plan, view of the entrance and the swimming pool.

Details of the exterior and views of the interior and the swimming pool.

Doussot house

Rudy Ricciotti
Bandol, Var, 1987
260 m²
Concrete, white rendering, tiled floors.

On a sloping site, the house develops along an axis of symmetry. The bedrooms are on the first floor, with the living room and kitchen on the ground floor. A second progression leads from the garden to the swimming pool, and then to the terrace and so to the house itself, connecting the exteriors to the inside of the dwelling.

On a winding, serpentine plot, the house turns its back on the road to open an entirely glazed facade to westwards. The first views – columns and open porches to the east, balconies to the south and terrace to the west – emphasise the value of the simple geometry of the built volume. In the same way, the little movements away from this – the pillar of the terrace, the curve of the balconies and the kitchen – oppose the rigour of the symmetrical layout.

A flight of stairs leads from the main entrance down to the garden below, the house taking on the role of filter, a necessary transitional space, between courtyard and garden. It assumes possession of a narrow site and models it in its entirety.

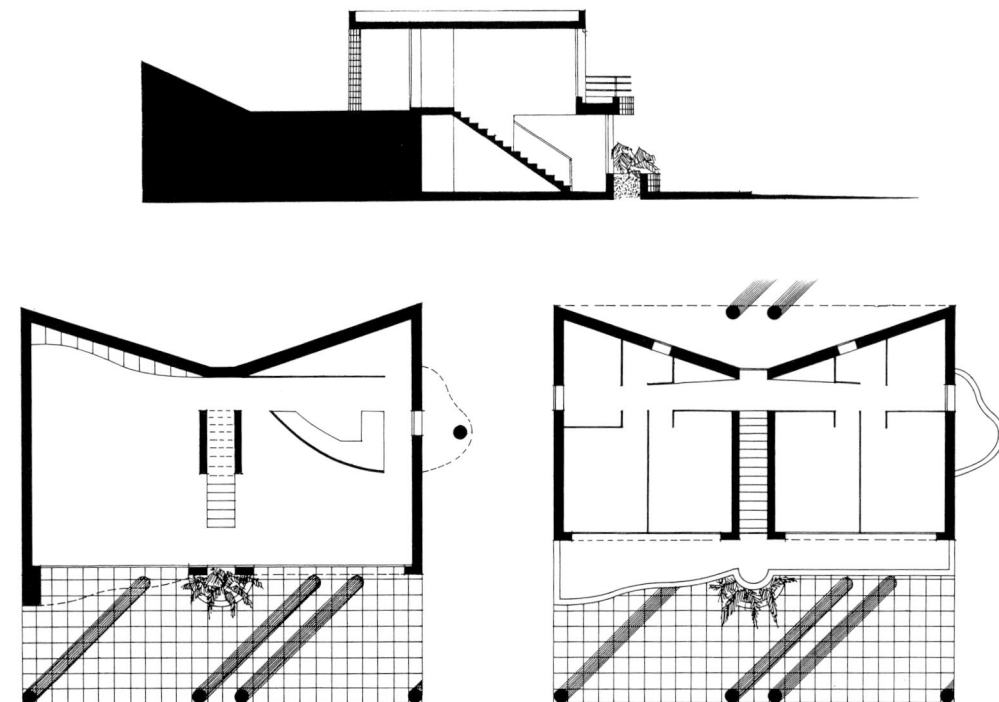

Section, plan and view of the exterior.

Detail of the entrance and the balcony, views of the interior and view of the main facade and the swimming pool.

Mancini house

C.C.D. (Gérard Cerrito / Xavier Chabrol / Régis Daniel)
Marseille, Bouches-du-Rhône, 1984
200 m²
Rough-shuttered concrete, pontoon terrace of Iroko wood.

On a steeply sloping site, this house is sheltered from the Mistral wind, all the rooms opening instead onto Marseille's harbour. The succession of terraces constitutes a series of promontories which traverse the site. Set back, against the rock, the various functions of the cubic volume are laid out over three levels – entrance hall, kitchen, living room and dining room on the ground floor, bedrooms on the first floor, and study and master bedroom on the top floor. A structured void on the first floor gives a spaciousness to the living room and dining room. The secondary volumes are aligned on the limits of the plot, reinforcing the main volume of the building. The exterior staircases connect the terraces with the natural terrain... At the back of the site the house rests against supporting walls which are of great importance in constituting its base and structuring the site where it gives onto the roadway. The volume of the swimming pool finds its natural location amongst the outcrops of rock. The overall form here – with access from below to a sloping site – invites comparison with the Doussot house, with its access from above.

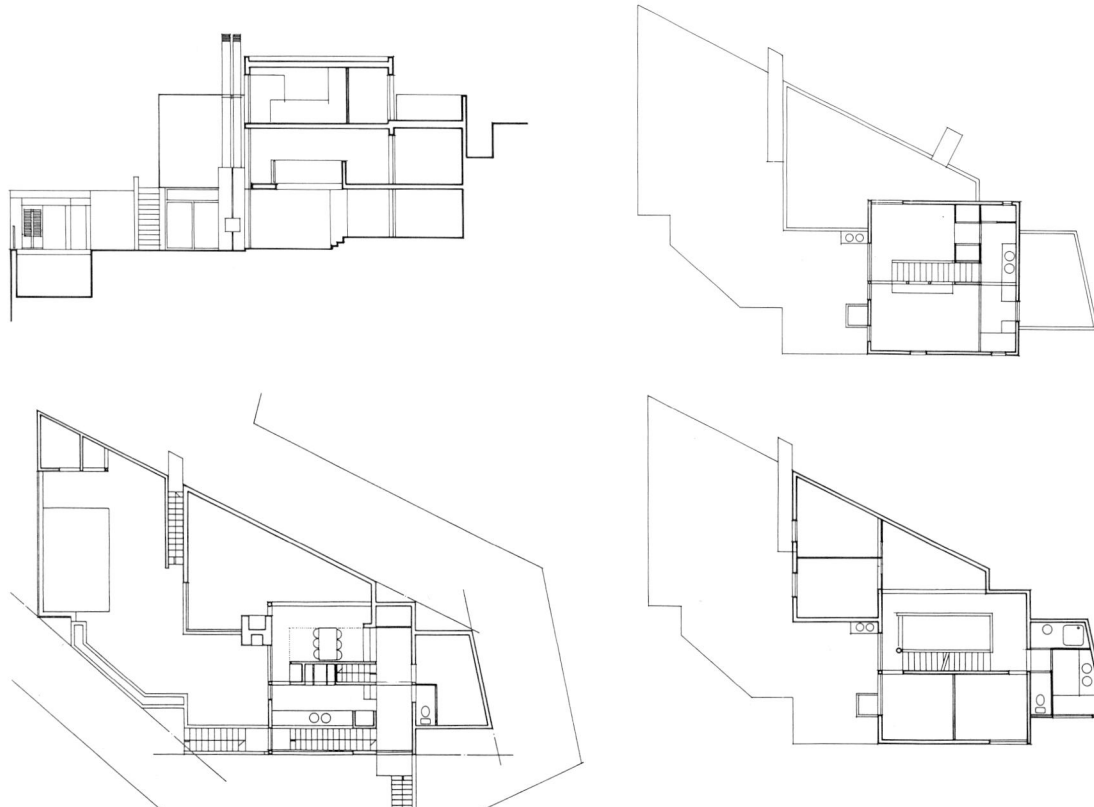

Plans, section and view of the exterior.

Views of the exterior.

Views of the terrace, the swimming pool and interiors.

Private house

Emmanuelle Colboc
Caseneuve, Vaucluse, 1987
140 m²
Concrete, rendering, pine flooring.

Situated between a volume which is slightly detached from the ground (intented for guests) and the main volume, articulated around a courtyard, the entrance acts as a point of distribution and interconnection. The subtle play of openings frames the landscape, carefully ensuring that the sun's rays do not enter the house. The main bays open onto the courtyard, sheltered from the heat of the day. The split-level living room and the kitchen opening onto the accessible roof terrace are the most clearly individual elements in the programme here. The double-depth treatment of the facades particularises certain zones, and the planes of the walls extend – in a line from the entrance to the corner of the living room – or intersect – guests' rooms, bathrooms – in order to counterpoint the volumes. The extremely horizontal distribution in this house is based around a broken axis. The variety of different openings gives each space its own unique character. Its simplicity and refinement make this project a model for the handling of a programme for a private house.

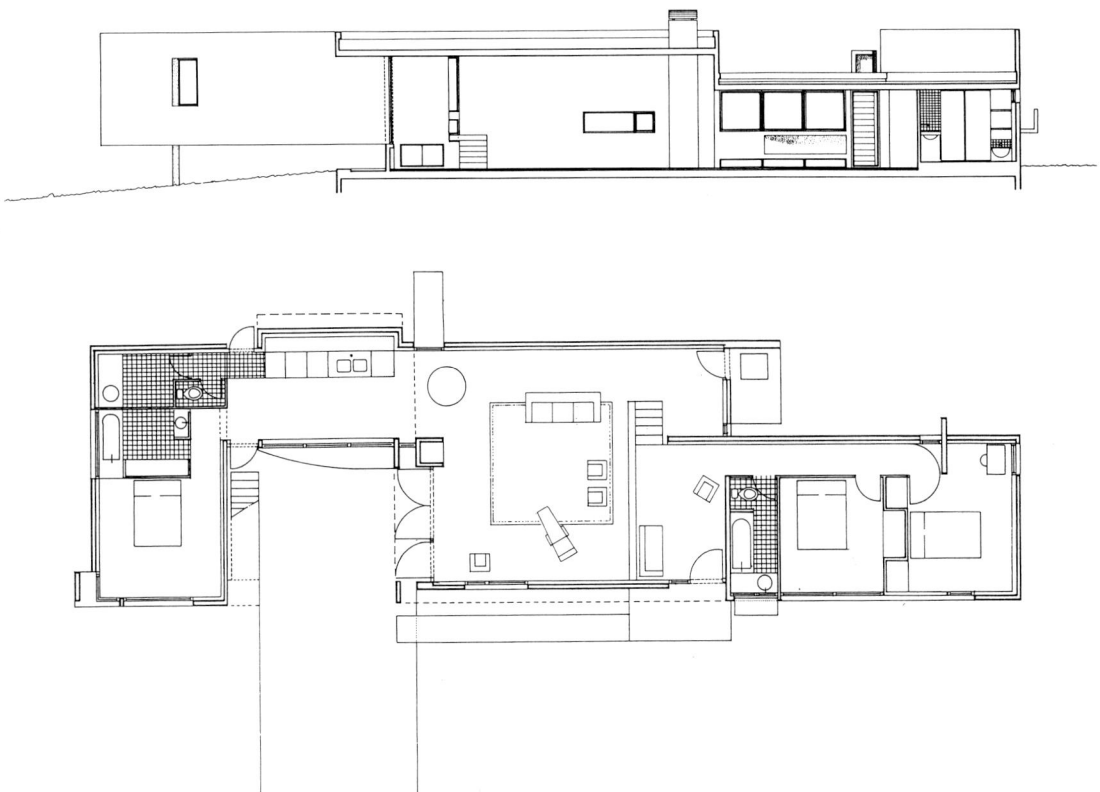

Section, plan and views of the exterior.

Previous pages: detail of the entrance and various views of the exterior.

Views of the kitchen and the living room.

Sauzet house

Maurice Sauzet
Sanary, Var, 1975
245 m²
Masonry, wood, terracotta, tiles.

Maurice Sauzet worked in the office of Jungo Sakakura, a disciple of Le Corbusier's, in Osaka for two years. His house recalls the moving space characteristic of Zen temples. The house "multiplies the states which participate within and without". The organisation is governed by displacement, with an interior/exterior ambiguity which both offers and conceals itself.

Three blocks with complex geometries (kitchen, dining room, bedrooms and services) are drawn together and hold each other at a distance around the courtyard and the living room, a space whose glazed window bays leave it entirely open in two directions. The main rooms of the house fan out along the south facade and the steps of the staircase delicately adapt the building to the topography. This house-cum-village is built up on itself so as to more fully develop its complex, spiralling circulation routes.

The heart and soul of the project are symbolised by the fireside inglenook, a mystic, enclosed space composed of shadows. The perspective lines inherent in the house's geometry are mentally present, even if they have not been drawn. Thus the mystery is kept intact.

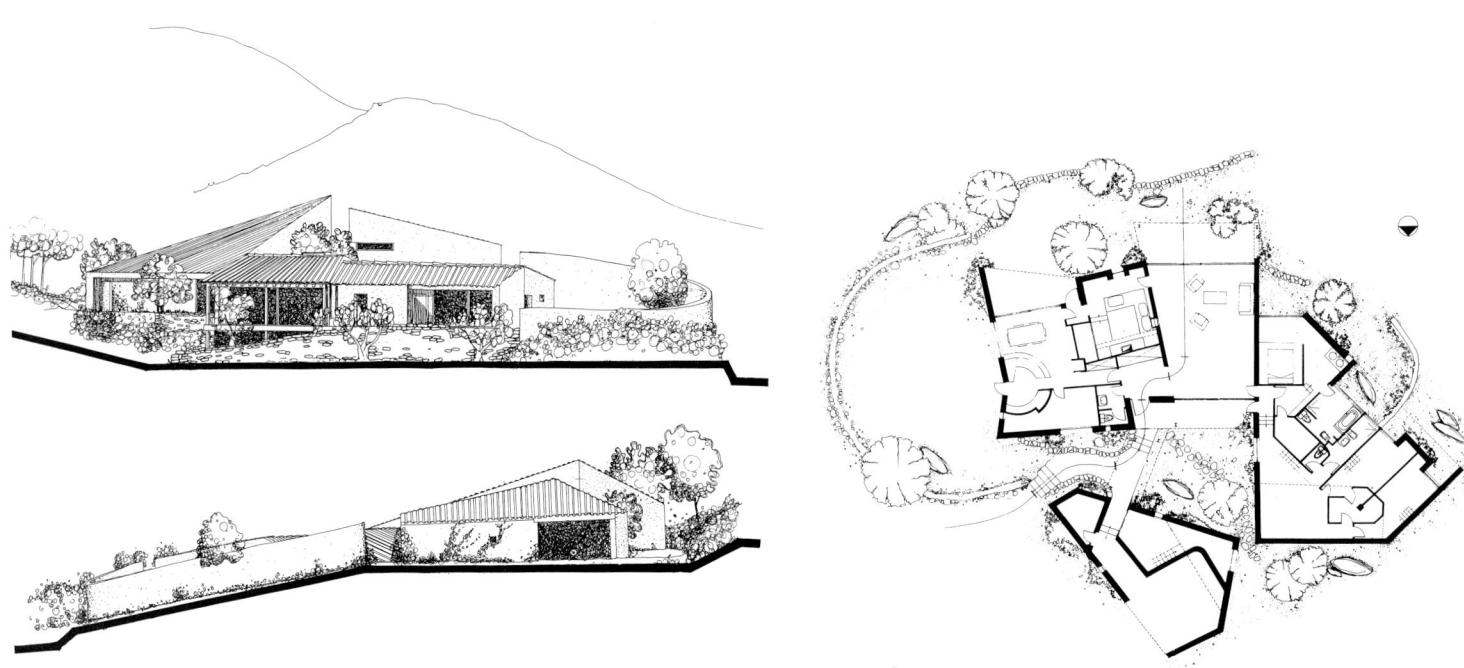

Plan, elevations and view of the exterior.

Detail of the porch and the terrace, view of the interior and partial views of the exterior.

Coppens house

Rudy Ricciotty
Bandol, Var, 1988
150 m²
Concrete structure 3 m units.

This fractured volume on a corner plot creates a series of spaces overlooking the town. An independent studio on the ground floor and a large gallery to the south are the functional particularities of this house.
Highly compact, the absence of usable outdoor space at ground level in this urban project is compensated for by terraces on the first floor and roof.
The rigour of the construction system is counterbalanced by the main volume's numerous additions and protuberances. The vertical circulation system is dual, interior and exterior, thus serving to open the building up to its surroundings. The volumetry is supported on the plane of the great north-west wall, against which the secondary volumetries break.
A powerful contrast is established between the minor opening in the north, east and west facades, and their multiplicity on the south facade, where the volume is fragmented into parallel planes.

Plans, elevations and views of the exterior.

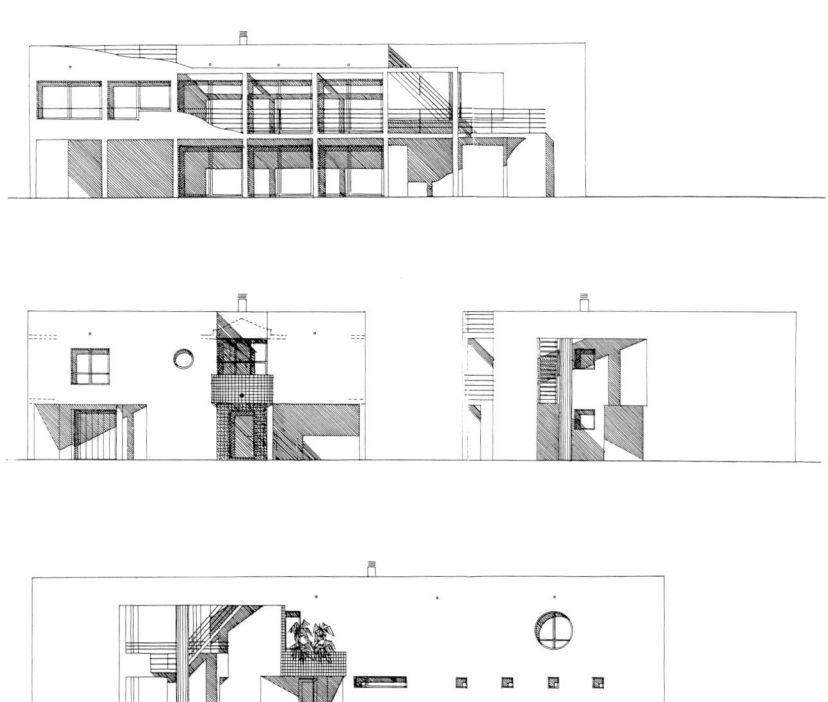
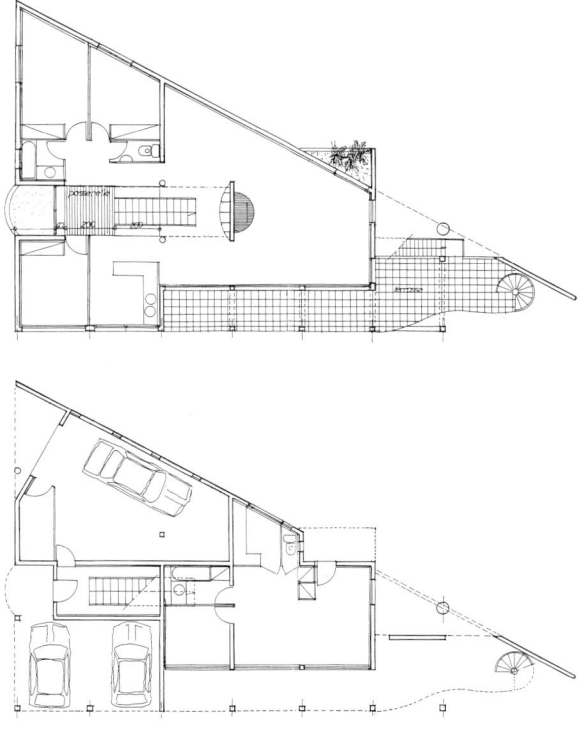

Views of the exterior.

Partial views of the exterior and
view of the interior.

Jaubert house

Gaston Jaubert
Pélissanne, Bouches-du-Rhône, 1970
375 m²
Rough-shuttered concrete, terracotta floors.

This house on two levels rigourously exploits the form of the triangle. The richness of the exterior detailing animates the surfaces in counterpoint to the two-dimensional dynamism of the triangular plan.

The right angle of this isosceles triangle, pointing to the north, gives protection against the effects of the Mistral.

The main access on the ground floor passes between outbuildings, the library and the garage, by way of a short flight of steps, clearly contrasted with the spacious volumes of the main rooms on the first floor.

The dining room is by the entrance, in keeping with Provençal tradition.

The regularity of the rhythm of the south facade is interrupted on the exterior by a gargoyle and the double sequence of the roofed terrace off the living room. In the interior, the plan opens or closes some of its cells, creating a destructured, moving space in opposition to the assertive geometry of the composition. A small courtyard-garden walls in part of the landscape for the private enjoyment of the house's occupants.

Plans, section and general view of the house and its surroundings.

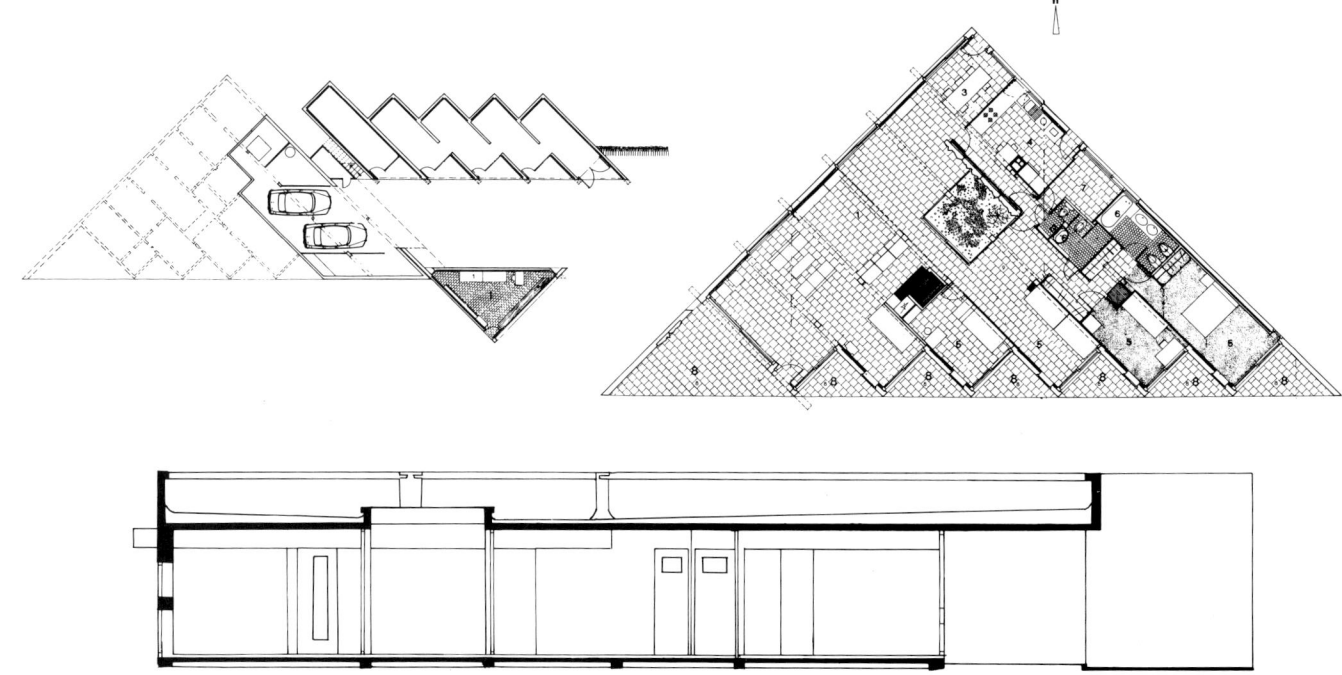

Partial views of the exterior and views of the interior.

"Arakao" house

Jacques Gautier
Roussillon, Vaucluse, 1985
270 m²
Partition walls, rendering, terracotta floors,
Lacoste stone, wooden flooring in the bedrooms.

The panoramic view from this belvedere house extends from Gordes to Apt, Lacoste and Bonnieux. This introspective house – only the narrow slit of the terrace which opens off the living room communicates with the exterior – bears the name "Arakao", meaning "crab's claws" in Tuareg. The extremely effective split-level plan in organised around a double flight of stairs which connects the bedrooms on the first floor with the communal spaces on the ground floor. The openings to the exterior – apart from the bay window in the living room – are of very reduced dimensions, framing views rather than creating a symbiosis between exterior and interior. Segments of a circle and the displacement of the grid by 45° from its true axis give dynamism to the basic cubic volume.

The house follows the sloping topography of the terrain to embed its entrance facade in the side of the hill.

From shade to light, the landscape – concealed during the entrance sequence – reveals itself once the visitor has entered the house.

Plans, elevations and view of the house and its surroundings.

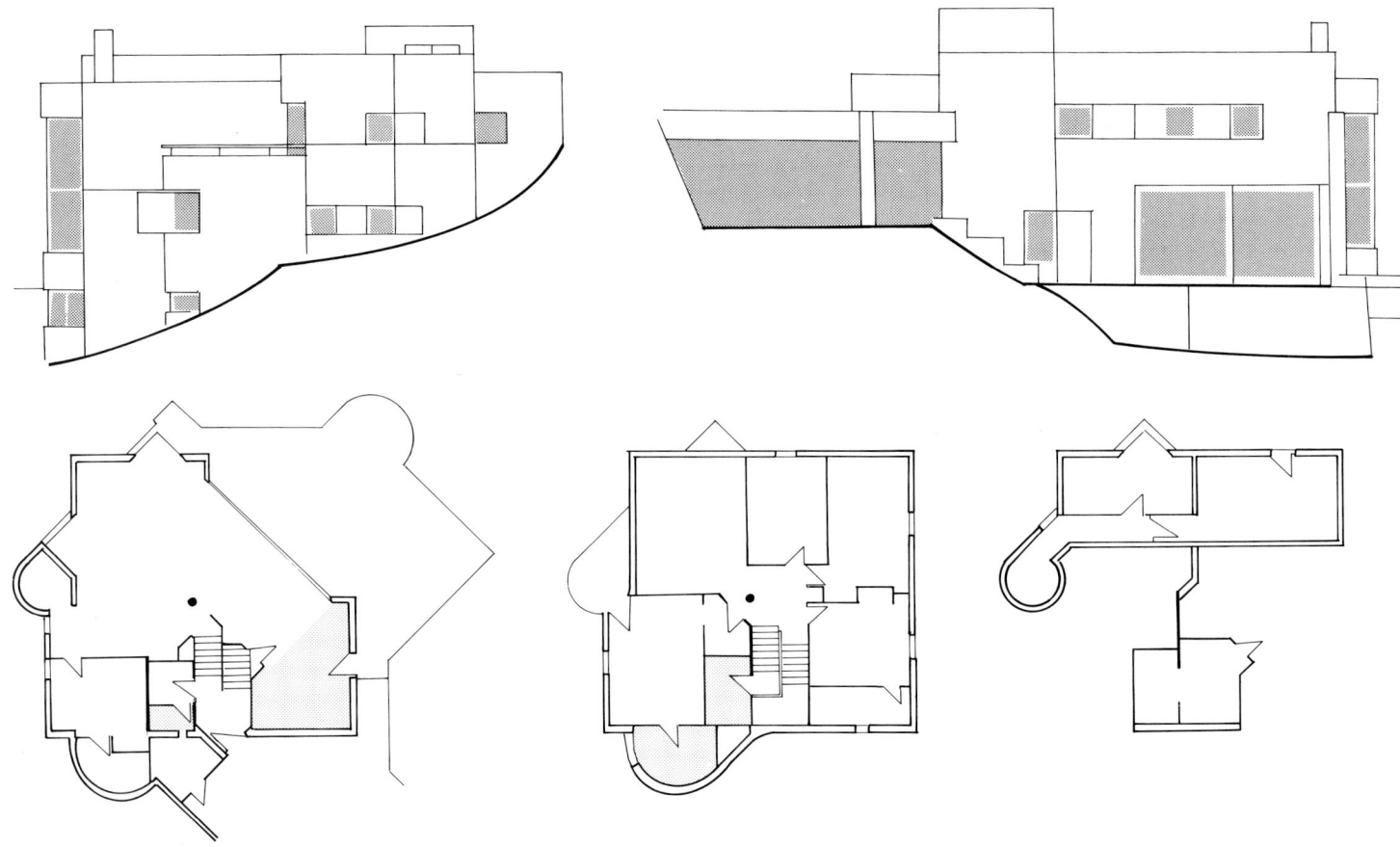

Detail of the terrace and the belvedere and various views of the exterior.

Following pages: views of the interior and detail of the exterior entrance to the terrace.

Mahaux house

Rudy Ricciotti
Nice, Alpes-Maritimes, 1988
180 m²
Concrete pillars, roof of channel tiles, white rendering.

From canopy roof to terrace to swimming pool, this uni-directional south-facing house follows the contours of the terrain and dominates the site through its longitudinal organisation.

Exterior constructions make up more than half the built surface. The simplicity of the plan's layout – enormous living room and kitchen on the ground floor, a linear sequence of bedrooms upstairs – is counterbalanced by the formal complexity of the multiple structures which it underpins. A basic 3.5 m grid sets the spatial rhythm, its regularity broken by the main entrance in the wall on the east-west axis. In similar fashion a central 1.0 m sequence on the north-south axis marks the entrance to the house. The very gently sloping roof with its channel tiles –probably in compliance with local building regulations – hides behind a parapet in order to conserve the modern character of the project. The play of balustrades, stairs, handrails and porthole windows marks this architecture as a continuation of the Latitude 43 project, inspired by the aesthetics of the steamboat.

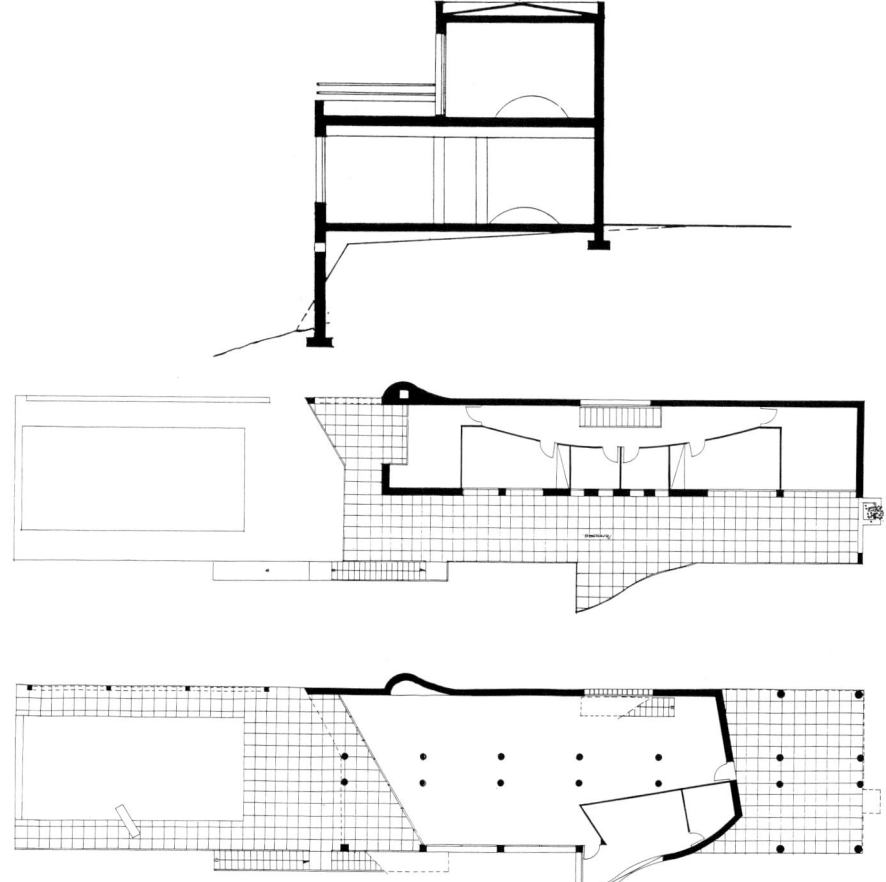

Section, plan and view of the exterior.

Previous pages: details of the exterior and the swimming pool.

Partial views of the exterior and detail of the interior.

Gleize house

François Clavel
Nimes, Gard, 1982
250 m²
Rough-shuttered concrete, wooden floor, use of the colour blue as leitmotif.

This cascading house is articulated around a triple-flight staircase which leads down from the entrance to an upper group of bedrooms to the kitchen-dining room, a double-height living room, and then to the three main bedrooms in the lowest part of the house.

The living room is extended out onto a terrace, constructed over the lower bedrooms, which overlooks the swimming pool below. The main bedrooms are divided into two sub-spaces with bed and night table on a raised platform by the entrance, a distribution space in line with the glazed bays. The fitted wardrobes are situated in a corridor-cum-dressing room which leads to the bathrooms. The entrance overlooks a landscaped interior garden. The light is structured between the openings of the glazed bays and the solids of the concrete walls. The volumes of the house are framed between the background of mature trees and the foreground of undulating thickets which dissolve the built mass in a integration with the setting which is full of surprises.

Plans, elevations and view of the exterior.

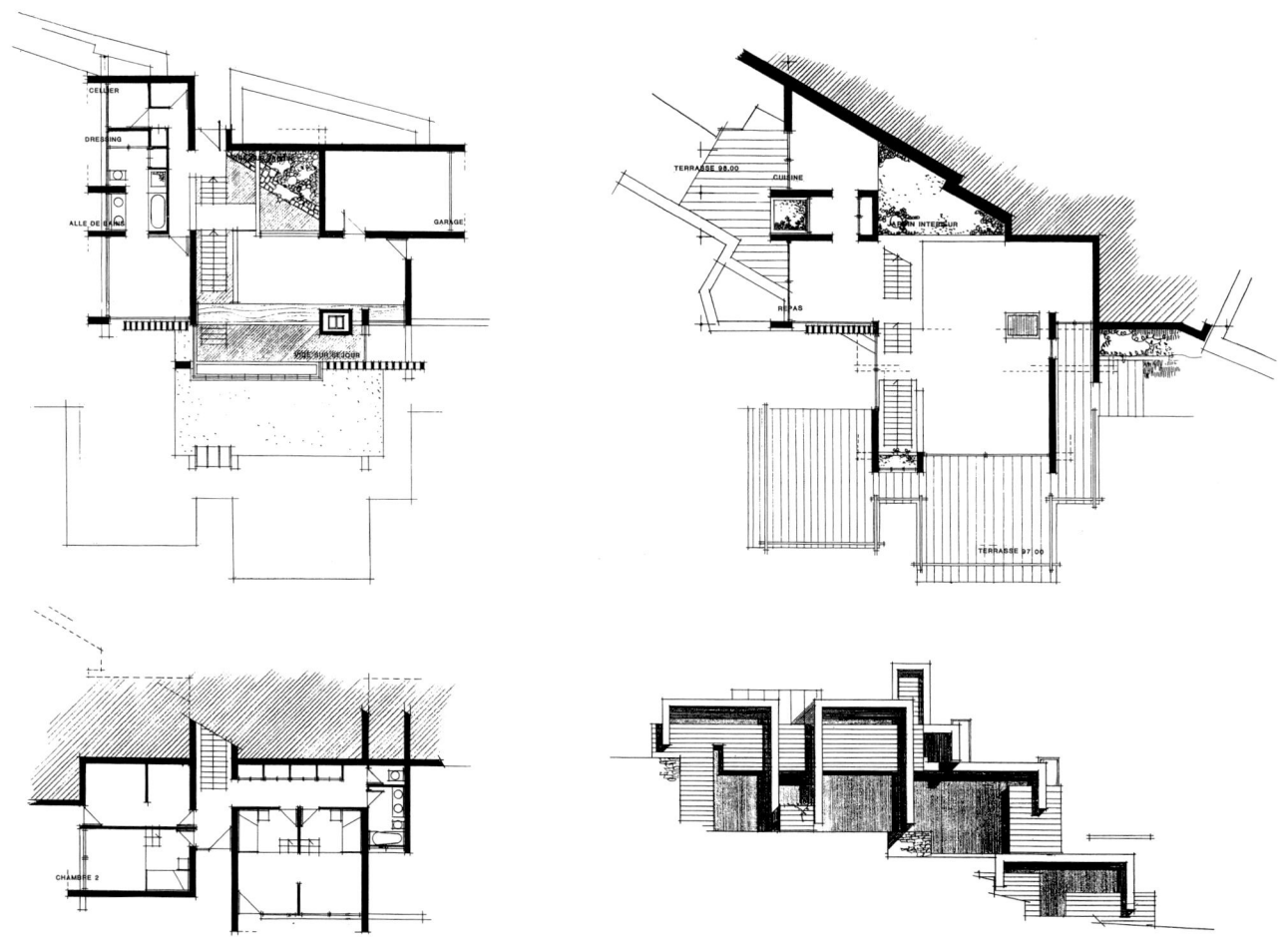

Views of the exterior and the interior.

131

View of the bathroom and the swimming pool.

Private house

Guy Grégori
Castelnau-le-Lez, Hérault, 1982
190 m²
Partition walls and rendering.

This squat "everyday object" without roof ridges is compactly concentrated on its site. The traditional distribution (living room on the ground floor, bedrooms on the first) opens out onto a succession of south-facing terraces.

The labyrinthine central circulation system is developed over four half-levels from the garage to the master bedroom, with the entrance at a halfway point in this layout. The various autonomous additions to the structure – chimneys and ventilation ducts, the lightwell over the staircase, the guttering – encourage a more thorough reading of the basic volume. In the same way, its symmetries seem to establish themselves, only to dissolve on a more attentive study of the plan. The mass of the house is effectively composed of the aggregation of fragmentary volumes linked together by the uniformity of the outer skin (coloured rendering).

The project nevertheless overhangs the ground it occupies, albeit rigorously framed within the limits of the plot.

Neither parallel with nor perpendicular to the slope of the site, it develops around the fictive centre of an axis.

Axonometric sketch, plans and view of the exterior from the garden.

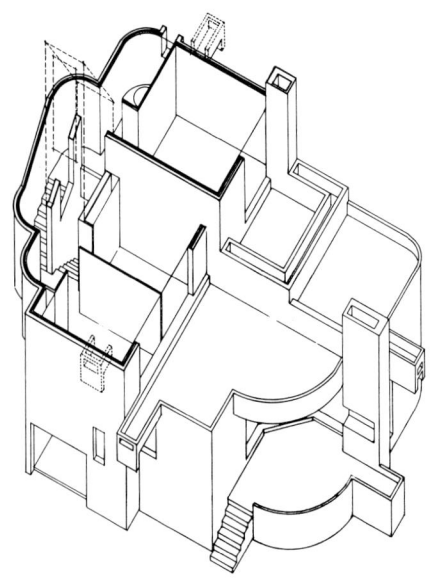
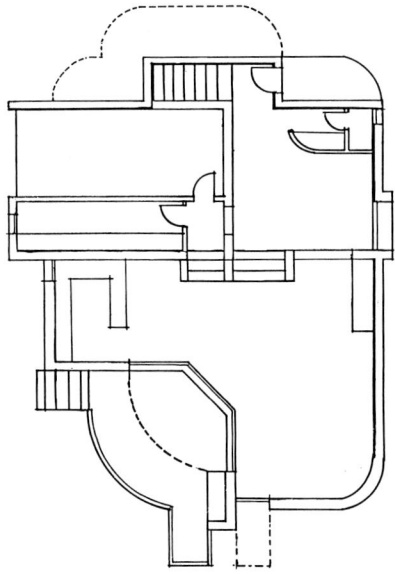
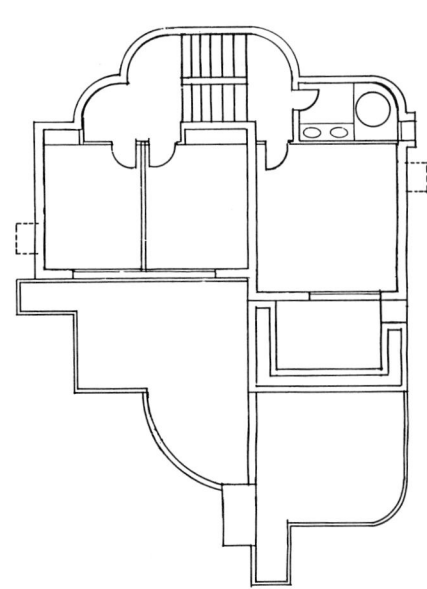

Details of the exterior.

Private house

Roland Simounet
Toulon, Var, 1975
600 m²
Partition walls, concrete.

The spaces of the house fit together to form a whole which is then engulfed by the surrounding vegetation. In the richness and ambiguity of its distribution, the house resembles a little enclosed village.

The cells of the numerous bedrooms are organised around a multiple central space. One exceptional quality of this project is its large surface area, in which it recalls the programme for the Noailles villa in Hyères.

The main openings are framed within niches set into the walls, in contrast to the secondary windows set flush with the walls. These are designed to slide back into the double partition walls, creating complete transparency between the house and its environment.

The numerous changes in level give an individual character to each space. The sophisticated treatment of the circulation and the special care devoted to the lesser spaces (niches, changes in the line of the walls, ...), create a secondary order which establishes a harmonious relationship between the extremely extensive programme and the people who use it.

Section, plan and view of the exterior and the entrance.

Details of the exterior and view of the studio from the exterior.

Views of the interior and the terrace.